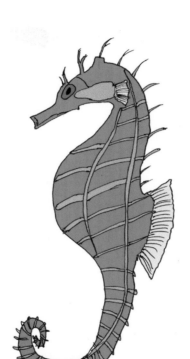

Sandy Grip

Billy Sharp

Hugh Hermit

Ben Clipper

The Captain

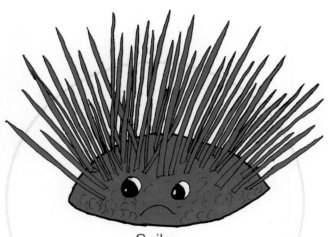

Spike

Nipper Sidewalker

Peter Sidewalker

Katie Pincher

Janet
Sidewalker

Susie Lightsfoot

Mr Crab,
the Headmaster

Thanks to Jo for your help and support.

Welcome to Lower Mudeford. Today we are going to share in the fun and games of **Crab Lines!**

Now crab lines are a big adventure in Lower Mudeford. What happens is the people from the world above, who are called human beings, come along to Mudeford Quay for a day out or sometimes a holiday. They have this great event where the mums and dads buy their children a crab line each. It's supposed to be a game for the children but to tell you the truth I think the mums and dads quite enjoy it as well.

First they buy bags of small pieces of fish, Tuna is the best, which they put on the ends of the lines. The children then try to catch the inhabitants of Lower Mudeford. Well they think that they catch them, but of course it is a great game for the crabs as well!

The crabs have their own rules for the game, like taking turns on going up on the lines, and the young crabs are not allowed to play until after school is finished.

When the children, (and sometimes the mums and dads), catch a crab they put them in their bucket. There is a lot of competition among the children about who can fill the bucket first, the crabs quite enjoy this part too and they have a real giggle and joke as they clamber over each other.

Today, down in Lower Mudeford, the crabs are up bright and early. It is Saturday, the spring sunshine is starting to warm up the sea, but more importantly it will bring out the holiday makers. Today should be a perfect day for playing Crab Lines.

The three young Sidewalkers are getting so excited, Mrs Sidewalker decides that they need some sea air to calm them down.

"When you have finished your breakfasts, I think you should go outside and see how many crabs are going to join you in your games today."

"Oh yes please," said Nipper. This is his first season of being allowed on the crab lines and he can't wait to get going. Janet and Peter smiled at their little brother. "Come on then Nipper, let's see who we can find," said Peter, "Janet why don't you go down to Sandy Bottom and call on your friends? You could knock on Miss Claw's door to see if she is coming today. We will all meet at the bottom of the sea wall."

"Ok," laughs Janet, "today is going to be a great day."

"Peter, can I go and see if Ben Clipper is coming? He is such fun - I hope he can come," says Nipper. "Good idea," said Peter, "I'll go up to the school house and see if I can persuade Mr Crab to come too. We will meet at the sea wall at ten O'clock."

"Bye!" shouts Nipper and scuttles off across the sand towards Ben's old Mussel Shell house on the right hand side of the village by the sea wall.

As Nipper pushes through the thick kelp he comes to the big rock, just before Ben Clipper's house, he sees something strange. The sand is moving. What on earth is that, thinks Nipper? The tip of an old sea shell starts to appear from the sand. "Oh it's Hugh Hermit, lovely to see you again," he says.

"Shush!" whispers Hugh, "Spike that nasty Sea Urchin is blocking my way into the village, I don't want to have my legs spiked."

Nipper peered around the rock and there he was, Spike the Sea urchin, with all of his spikes bristling with the movement of the water.

"Wait there Hugh," whispers Nipper, "I'll go and get Ben Clipper he'll know what to do, and off he scurries."

Hugh Hermit is a traveller. He is never in one place very long but everybody in the village likes him, and they all look forward to his return so they can listen to all of the tales he has to tell.

Hugh originally comes from Tenby in West Wales, but he likes to spend his life travelling along the coast from West Wales to the South of England. The sea shell that he carries on his back is his little house, which suits him fine to be able to stop where ever he is on his journeys and his house is always with him.

Nipper arrives at Ben Clipper's, out of breath and looking even pinker than he normally does. Ben looks out of the window and sees him puffing loudly.

"Hey young Nipper, what is it that has got you so out of breath like that?" says Ben. "Oh Ben," says Nipper, "You must come quickly. Hugh has come to visit, but Spike has got him trapped behind the big rock and won't let him pass. Please help!"

"Calm down Nipper," said Ben, "I'll soon sort out that Sea Urchin, his spikes will be a lot less spiky once my files have done their job. He will be Spike in name only."

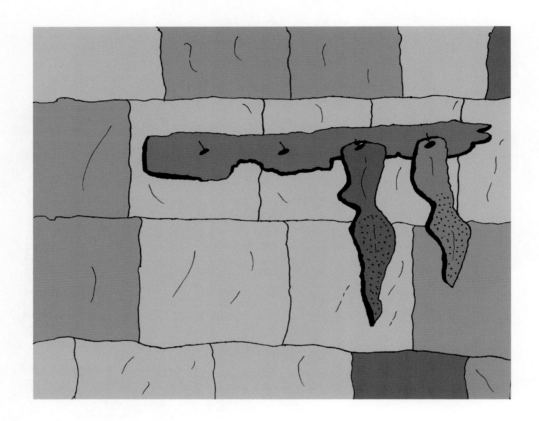

Ben grabs two of his biggest files from the wall outside his workshop and off he goes following Nipper to the big rock.

As they approach the rock Ben sees Hugh doing his best to frighten Spike away.

"Hello Hugh, it's good to see you again, I understand that our friend Spike here needs some work doing on his spikes, they are getting a bit long, aren't they Spike?"

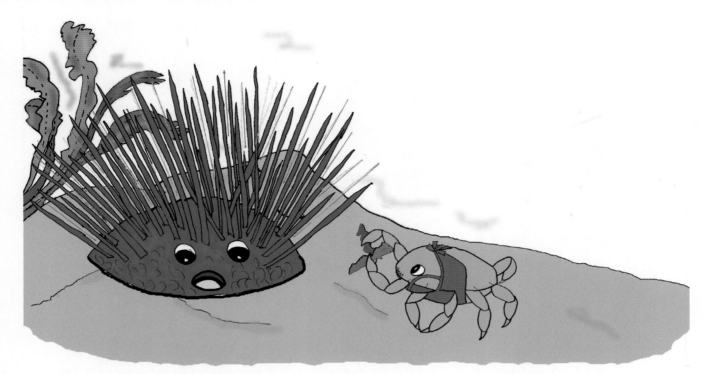

Spike looked round and saw Ben marching towards him with a long file in each of his front claws. He squealed with fright and his spikes went stiff as he thought what those files would do to his beautiful spikes. He had to get out of here quickly. With a huge jump he leapt off the rock and was swept away by a wave into the deep sea and away from the village.

They all laughed, "Well done Ben," said Hugh, "I've never seen a sea urchin look so frightened. Thank you Nipper for coming to my rescue and bringing back Ben, what a clever young crab you are."

Nipper felt himself swell up with pride. "It's a good job I was passing," said Nipper, "I was coming to ask Ben if he would like to come up on the Crab Lines today, but now I can ask you both."

"I think that is a wonderful idea," said Hugh, "What about you Ben, do you think you can find some time as well?"

"Yes", said Ben, "It's time I had some fun again, I've been working very hard recently,"

So off went the three of them, with Nipper leading the way and Ben and Hugh walking behind, talking about old times.

When they got to the Sea Wall it was packed with crabs all waiting for the lines to start coming down with lots of juicy bait on. Nipper ran on ahead to find Janet and Peter and to tell them all about the adventure with Spike the Sea Urchin.

Janet called to him and he ran to join them. Janet had got some school friends with her, Susie Lightsfoot and Katie Pincher, but Miss Claw couldn't make it today as she needed to do some shopping. Susie is Miss Sally Lightsfoot's (the PE teacher) sister and Katie is Dr Pincher's daughter. Peter had talked Mr Crab into coming and two of his friends as well, Billy Sharp and Sandy Grip. Billy is P.C. Sharp's son.

They all laughed at Nipper's story. "Well done Nipper you certainly seem to have a way of getting into adventures", said Mr Crab, "I would like you to write it down and read it to the school on Monday morning."

"Yes Mr Crab, I'll do it this evening," said Nipper.

Just then,
someone spotted
the crab lines
coming down
into the water.

"Here they come"

The crabs all rushed
to jump and cling onto
the fish bait, and then felt themselves being pulled up
through the water to the land above.

Peter, Billy and Sandy race each other to the line on
the left. Sandy jumped towards a fat juicy piece of
fish, making it look easy - as his name 'Sandy Grip'
suggests!

"Come on you two," he called to Peter and Billy, who
were both trying to catch hold of the end of the line.

Peter jumped again and managed to catch hold, then with Sandy holding onto his front claw, he stretched down with his back legs so that Billy could reach him and pull himself up. Then they felt the line move and they were on their way, slowly being pulled up through the water to the world above.

"Wow!" shouted Billy, "This is great fun."

Once there, the children start to laugh with joy, as they pull the crabs gently off of the lines and put them in their buckets.

Ben Clipper and Nipper are both in a bucket at the moment, Nipper is wriggling and clambering over everyone. "Hey Nipper," shouts Ben, "Your claws could do with filing, come and see me when you get home and I'll do something about them." "OK Ben" calls Nipper, "Oh by the way have you seen Janet, she was on the next line to me on the way up but I haven't been able to find her since?" "No I can't say that I have," said Ben, "but I'll tell you what, why don't you and I climb out of here and see if we can find her?" "Oh yes," squeals Nipper, that will be great fun." "Right then," said Ben, "You climb onto my back, and I'll climb onto those two crabs, then you should be able to reach the handle and when you're out you can hang on with your front claws and I'll pull myself up on your back legs."

So they started to climb over a small crab, it was Billy, Peters friend. "Hi Billy" said Nipper "We're looking for Janet have you seen her?" "I think I saw her on the last line on the right" said Billy. On the first two attempts to get out of the bucket Nipper couldn't quite reach the handle, but on the third go Ben stretched up as high as he could and Nipper got a hold. He pulled up hard and then he was there. Now it was Ben's turn. Nipper took a firm hold of the handle and let his legs hang back into the bucket, Ben grabbed hold and started to claw his way up. Oh it was hard for Nipper after all he is only a tiny little crab, and Ben is one of the biggest crabs in the village, Ben was about half way up when Nipper felt his grip starting to go.

"Oh no I mustn't let go," thought Nipper. He felt his left claw slipping, he gripped tightly for a few more seconds and then it fell away, "Ah!" He squealed in pain as he hung on bravely with his right claw." "Nearly there," said Ben as he pulled himself up onto the top of the bucket, then they both slithered down the outside and onto the ground.

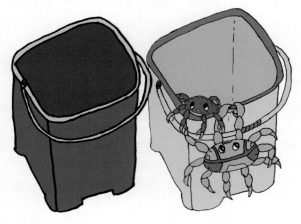

"My oh my, you're a brave little crab if ever I met one," said Ben, "If you can do that now, just imagine what you'll be able to do when you're my age."

Nipper giggled a little and he felt very proud, because praise from Ben was praise indeed.

"Right, let's get on with finding this sister of yours Nipper, before it's time for the finish." said Ben, and off they went together. What a sight they looked too, the smallest and the largest crab in the village running along the seawall side by side.

"Janet, Janet are you there?" cries Nipper as he comes to the next group of buckets, No reply.

"Janet are you in there?" calls Ben as he taps the side of another bucket with his large front claw, still no reply. But a large claw appeared over the top of the bucket. It was the Captain. "She is in the next bucket I think." said the Captain.

"Thanks Captain." says Ben.

Nipper spots a very large bucket over to the right, "Let's try that one Ben," he shouts as races towards it. He taps lightly on the bottom of the bucket, "Hello Janet, Janet are you in there?" he calls gently.

"Hulou, Hulou", comes a muffled reply, "I'm stuck right at the bottom," Janet manages to say, before a large crab clambers on top of her, and stops conversation for a bit.

"Quick Ben," shouts Nipper running back towards him, "How can we help Janet to get out?"

"It's alright Nipper don't panic," said Ben, "I've just heard two of those human beings talking, and it's nearly time for the finish. She will get out then."

Then comes the <u>finish!</u>

When the buckets are full, the children stand back from the seawall and tip the buckets out. The race is on! Off they go, some bumping into each other, some going the wrong way. No they have got it right now, heading for the sea.

Now the first crab reaches the edge of the sea wall.
It's Mr Crab the teacher, will he be brave enough to
make the jump, he stops and takes a look. Oh it's a
long way, he's not sure. Then a young crab rushes
past him, he gives a big squeal and leaps off the edge,
it is Sandy, Peter's friend. Splash! He hits the water
and then he gently floats back to Lower Mudeford.

This makes up the mind of Mr Crab. He's not going to be outdone by a youngster. So he takes a big breath, pushes off with his back legs and he's gone.

Splash, plop, splash, splash, crabs are hitting the water all around and then floating back home laughing and giggling on the way down, telling each other their tales of the day's adventure.

Now it's time for the big bucket that Janet's in. A little girl picks it up and takes it to the back of the path, as far from the sea wall as she possibly can. Then she gently tips it up and all of the crabs come tumbling out. They all look a bit bemused, Janet is wandering around in circles and that's when Nipper spots her. He runs towards her and grabs hold of her claw with his.

"Come on Janet," he cries, "I'll race you to the sea."

"Ooh Nipper," she laughs, "You made me jump."

"Oh not yet Janet," he giggles, "save your jump until you get to the sea wall."

They both burst out laughing and rush towards the sea. "Hey wait for me you two." calls Ben as he runs after them. They all reach the edge of the wall together and stop to have a quick look. "Gosh, the sea is almost to the top of the wall", said Janet. "Yes it's high tide now." said Ben.

"Right," said Ben

"We'll all jump together, after three.
One, two, three."

SPLASH!

They all hit the water almost together, and slowly float
down to Lower Mudeford. Nipper is proudly telling his
sister of his tale of how Ben and himself got out of the
bucket, and Ben backs up his story. Janet smiles to
herself, and thinks how lucky she is to be part of this
lovely community.

When they arrive back on the sea bed of Lower Mudeford Janet spots her two friends, Katie and Susie. She rushes over to see them. Katie was laughing and Susie looked a bit dazed by everything.

"What's so funny?" asked Janet.

"Oh it's Susie" laughs Katie, "She looked so funny when she landed with her hat pushed down over her eyes. Go on Susie, you tell Janet, I can't stop laughing."

Susie pushed her hat straight and began to see the funny side to it. "Well," she said, "I was in a bucket and I heard Ben calling for you Janet. I was going to answer, but then the Captain, who hadn't seen me at the bottom, reached up so that he could speak to Ben and stood on my hat with his back legs. I couldn't see a thing. Then when we were tipped out of the bucket the Captain realised what had happened and grabbed my claw and led me to the sea wall and helped me to get home. It was a bit of a shock but I can see how funny I must have looked."

They all laughed as they made their way home after a wonderful day playing Crab Lines.

Well time to go now, thank you for spending your day with us. It will soon be time for the inhabitants of Lower Mudeford to go on their Summer Holiday, so we look forward to seeing you soon for another adventure at Lower Mudeford.

Back to School

Come and spend some time in the Magical World of Lower Mudeford, share the fun and adventures of this little world of Crabs and sea life that lives beneath the waves.

It is the start of the summer term, but what adventures lie in wait for the young crabs of Lower Mudeford, when they meet their new P.E. Teacher.

Printed in Poland
by Amazon Fulfillment
Poland Sp. z o.o., Wrocław